Foreword

It's been a long ti   :ars have
tipped a global out   sed on a
paradigm shift that   my purpose and legacy? Ho   ly in this
'new normal'?

Diahanne nails our dilemma at its source, honing in on
the self-love methods she is already respected for; the
'Me-ology™' concept that she designed to change the world
from within ourselves as individuals.

Diahanne provides comfort food for the soul, peppered with
childhood memories and the flavoursome Caribbean sayings
she was raised on; the life-changing death of her mother is
explored alongside vignettes of discovery and learning. With
each chapter, the book becomes more intentional, focusing
on lessons learned, and how they can contribute to devising
a better future.

Contrary to this book's controversial title, this memoir is not
an opportunity for Diahanne to wax lyrical about herself, but
more an effort to infuse self-love, in the very same way that she
helps countless many in her daily life.

As a reader of this book, you cannot fail to be impacted by
Diahanne's journey. You may not have lived Diahanne's
experiences, but you will recognise them: painful choices,
longed-for love, the merciless tyranny of abuse and the

constancy of how much she attributes to the women whom shoulders she stands upon.

There is no doubt that for Diahanne, telling her story has been a labour of love. Having taken a truly extraordinary journey, she invites us along and, in doing so, opens our worlds to new possibilities.

Daniella Maison BA (Hons) MA

About the Author –
Dr. Diahanne Rhiney BCAe

I had to relearn to live, love, and let go – all over a short period of time. My life was significantly shattered as a result of surviving a murder attempt, and losing my mother, my 'soul-mate'. At a desperate time when I was in need, I had to contend with less. My fight for survival had begun. In this book I share my touching journey. One that I embraced with one focus in view: ME. I couldn't turn back the clock, I couldn't forget what happened, on occasions I couldn't even share what had happened to me – but now I could move forward. I'm a different person now, and I'm loving it. Thanks to the lessons I've learnt on my journey through life, and affectionately share in this book. I wish to acknowledge and thank my dad (who I don't remember him ever telling me 'no'…. ha ha!); my sister Claudette who has been my 'rock'); Daniella (my baby sister from another mother!); Veronica (for being that mother figure and mentor, and always being that point of reason with the occasional 'pepper mout'! Claudia (for being the epitome of real friendship); and for many others for giving, touching my life, expanding my circle of friendship and trust, being authentic and just being there! You have been, and continue to be, a tremendous support to me and helped this book become realized, written, and published. And, of course to the One above, for giving me the courage to speak, fight back and be heard. Finally, to Kevin, my knight in shining armour who I never believed existed and who accepts me for me. Mum - I live by your words of wisdom in this book and dedicate it especially to you. Xx

CONTENTS   **PAGE**

I can still feel the dark presence of someone stood behind me; the sick feeling in your gut when you know that danger is near. I can still feel the cool steel of the gun against the back of my head. There were no words, just an empty silence. Then, the trigger was pulled. My life flashed before my eyes; every single choice I'd made leading up to this moment lined up inside my mind and I knew in my heart this would be my very last moment.

I'm starting this book with what could have been the end because in many ways, it was...

Live with intention.
Walk to the edge.
Listen Hard.
Practice wellness.
Play with abandon.
Laugh.
Choose with no regret.
Appreciate your friends.
Continue to learn.
Do what you love.
Live as if this is all there is.

Mary Anne Radmacher

The first words of Mary Anne Radmacher's quote are vital to living an All About Me life... 'Live with intention'.

I suspect that you may have picked up this book wondering why I'd choose such a 'self-centred' title. After all, we've been led to believe that saying 'It's All About Me' is the height of selfishness.

It's not entirely untrue. If we go about our lives saying 'it's all about me' at the expense of others, we are probably completely self-absorbed; too focused on our own needs to think of anyone else. Being selfish; when your happiness comes at the cost of another's happiness, or you hurt others chasing your happiness, then the intention is usually toxic, and happiness will never be found.

This book uses the word YOU almost 1,000 times for good reason… it's all about…

"**YOU** YOURSELF **ARE** YOUR **OWN** **OBSTACLE** RISE ABOVE **YOURSELF**"

1. All About You

Selfish sɛlfɪʃ
adjective: selfish

1. of a person, action, or motive) lacking consideration for other people; concerned chiefly with one's own personal profit or pleasure.

So, here is where I'm going to be controversial. Your life is all about YOU. Here's the rub: the old saying 'it's not what you say but how you say it' applies here. In this case, it is the intention behind being self-centred. If we pull those words apart and look at them from a different angle, placing yourself at the centre of your life, being self-centred is a powerful life choice. The word centred creates thoughts of balance, steadiness and equilibrium. What could be more fulfilling than being truly self-centred?

Self-centred

1. independent of outside force or influence: self-sufficient
2. concerned with one's own needs or interests.

Intention is the proof of our motivation; it sets the pace on our journey towards the goal. Intention is quite literally the 'why' behind our actions. The 'why' behind All About Me is to be self-centred with the goal of living your life as a whole person and as fully as possible.

I want to explore the art of placing your happiness and wellbeing first. Giving yourself priority is your self-respect shining through which is why it's so important to be who you want to be, not what others want you to be. Living an authentic life that is positively self-centred and lived out from a place of wholeness, is what I like to call an 'All About Me' life, which I believe is the key to contentment. In a Nutshell...

This isn't just another self-help book filled with fads and fancy words that sound good but have no real meaning. 'All About Me' is an outpouring based on the tough lessons I have had to learn the hard way and the conclusions I have drawn.

Anyone who knows me will know that as much as I am very vocal about social and global issues, when it comes to talking about my private life, I am not nearly as loud! In putting this book together, I was torn, asking myself 'how much do I share?' I'm not part of the social media age who post(s) photos of my dinner so, I battled over how much to give away. I decided to share several key areas of my life with brutal honesty and with the sole intention of inspiring and empowering my readers. As you read this book you will start to see that it is actually All About YOU. Still, in sharing my insights and anecdotes, lessons learned and journey, I have taken a leap and shared some very intimate parts of my life.

Yes, I am a psychologist and a professional, but this book is based, first and foremost, on my experiences as a woman. I wear many hats (we will get into that later), but I haven't worn my psychologist hat in writing this book. I've simply written this as a woman. A woman who has lived, loved, lost, and learned.

I don't have all the answers, but I have learned a thing or two along the way and I truly hope that my lessons help you to realise your truth. We all have one; I'm still realising mine and appreciating what a beautiful journey it is. Join me as we go on this voyage of (self-centred) discovery together.

From domestic abuse to bereavement, there have been pivotal moments in my life when I have come to realise that if I do not pause and put myself first, I eventually lack the energy and wherewithal to be the mother, sister, daughter, aunty, friend, partner, businesswoman and woman that I know I can be. My mother's guidance has played a strong role in shaping my understanding of self-esteem because she lived a life that was so naturally 'Me-ology™'; she was a pioneer, a trailblazer who invested her knowledge in growing and helping others. She was also a proud Caribbean woman and so you'll notice this book is peppered with patois sayings. In this book, I share key moments of my life with you and explore how each one paved the way for my inner strength to ultimately grow, even though at the time I feared they would destroy me. I call these moments 'recollections' and the journeys they triggered my 'lessons learned'. Before we get started, I'd like you to look over and really reflect on these affirmations as they will form the bedrock of building an All About Me life.

I am alive and so I have worth
Saying no is not a negative thing
I'm human, not perfect
I'm ready to accept who I am:
the good and the bad
I want to feel good because of
me I am ready to start living a
life that is All About Me...

2. Me-ology™

Me-ology™ is the self-love conversation behind living an All About Me life that presents the concept of unearthing the truth about who we really are in order to be our best selves. In this book we are going to redefine what it is to lead a life that is all about YOU. That's why all the practices in this book are based on a concept I call Me-ology™.

Me-ology™ was created to help empower women and children all over the world by building *self-esteem*. It's my own take on empowerment; a way of life fused with a specific blend of sports psychology, mastery-oriented motivational climates, success mentalities and professional and personal experience.

Me-ology™ re-defines the pillars of *self-esteem* as the foundation of all the decisions you'll ever make, how you treat yourself, and how you allow others to treat you. Boundaries are more than just lines on a map. They are an essential toolkit for every area of our lives as new research demonstrates that self-respect is *crucial* for happiness.

Once we achieve true inner-strength and self-belief we can be the best version of ourselves. This in turn leads us to make better choices, overcome challenges with conviction, feel independently happy (whether we are alone or with others), and ultimately helps us to be a source of positive energy to our loved ones. As modern human beings, our self-esteem has been knocked in so many ways that it's hard to even spot anymore. Our standards for ourselves as women have slipped by the wayside somewhere. Self-belief is harvested and grown from inside, it's the power base of energy that we were born with. Most of us are unaware we have this power, this energy centre, from which all our self-belief and confidence grows; where our choices are taken, and actions are made.

The first step to achieving any goal in life is to develop the strengths within our character; domestic violence, abuse, bereavement, job dissatisfaction are all, to varying degrees, some of the experiences that cause our inherent power base to fade away. We become vulnerable, no matter how strong we appear on the surface, we begin to close doors and walk in fear.

Focusing on your holistic wellbeing is, in fact, the most self-less you can be when it is authentic, has a positive intention and benefits others.

Self-esteem is about how we value ourselves, our perceptions, and beliefs in who we are and what we are capable of. Our self-esteem can be misaligned with other people's perception of who we are; It's a fact that we teach people how to treat us and whether it's with family, friends, co-workers, or lovers.

"Tomorrow is promised to no-one so use your God given talent today."

Caroline Rhiney, mummy

Recollection

Some years ago, I was in an unhappy relationship. As an independent, strong, and focused woman I wasn't afraid to say to my ex-partner 'I'm unhappy, this isn't working for me, I need some time out.' Sensible? I thought so. Moments later, he pulled out a gun and tried to kill me. It was a major turning point. From that moment on I was stalked, threatened, and bullied. My life was constantly at risk. My confidence was knocked, and I lived my life in fear and shame. You see, I was raised to be a strong, independent, educated woman. I'm the daughter of a welterweight boxing champi- on and a formidable mother. I, like many others, presumed domestic violence was something that happened to 'other people'.

My greatest obstacle to freedom was my own overbearing feeling of shame. I lived a lie because I believed that if I spoke up, people who looked up to me and perceived me as a strong, capable, independent woman would see me as a fraud and as weak. I was afraid that all the things that had made me successful would be the very same reasons I might be disbelieved or misunderstood. It was after this experience that I realised that domestic abuse doesn't discriminate. I also realised that knowing who you are commands continuous work.

Now, I understand the power of minimisation and denial in domestic abuse but at the time I really didn't view myself as a victim. I tried to simply get up, brush off my knees and keep moving forward without realising this incident had shaped my life forever.

Even after my former partner had just tried to murder me, I didn't think I was a victim of domestic abuse. Why? Well because I believed that because I wasn't beaten or abused every day, I couldn't possibly be a victim of domestic abuse. I listened to other women's powerful stories and I believed they were more worthy because I got away.

My denial and several critical factors led to my delay in speaking up. It just never occurred to me that he didn't deserve my loyalty or concern. I didn't tell my family because I knew how much they loved me and that by telling them they'd be compelled to do something about it; I knew they'd be distressed and angry and, to me, that would have meant he had won. None of this protected me for the new feelings I had to encounter; new feelings that all abuse survivors know only too well. I had always been noticeably confident, and yet this new version of me was constantly looking over my shoulder. I felt paranoid, vulnerable, and violated. I avoided the area he lived in. I invested in security cameras and was careful about what I said to people in case he found out where I was and came back to finish what he started. I had a public profile and yet I retreated, dreading his attempts to contact me via social media. I worried for his new victims. I told my closest friends, as domestic abuse victims often do when we know in our gut that somebody wants you dead: 'If anything should ever happen to me… it's him.'It was a new type of fear and vulnerability I had never experienced. The moment the reality of what I had survived really hit me, I knew I had an obligation to speak out. I finally accepted that I had been a victim, and although I survived that night, denial hinders growth and I had to do more to be a true survivor. Accepting I was a victim and speaking out were the first steps in my personal victory. Speaking up when it's safe is a form of therapy. It has only been a few years since I have even told some of my family members, let alone delivering TEDX talks and writing articles, but the more I am honest about it is the more I feel empowered, it affirms that I have survived this and it gives me purpose to use my experience to help, educate and empower Domestic Abuse victims all over the world. I am no longer a victim; I am a victor.

Lessons Learned

Doing what you know is best for you is not always the easy path but ultimately, it is so worth it.It took me some time to realise that I would never return to who I once was if I didn't go back to focusing on my inner self. It wasn't easy, but I got there in the end. Now, I'm in a position to educate and inspire others with a charity called Strength With In Me: 'S.W.I.M' and it took a major investment of energy and time to be in this position, I really had to make my life 'All About Me.' Probably at least once a week I moan about 'buzzwords'; in the work that I do I hear lots of them.

I've spent several years bemoaning to my friends and in my articles about how words like 'diversity' and BAME have become a talking shop. I believe in affirmative action; find the heart of a problem and work on it to see a result.

The point at which words get overused because it's in fashion is usually the point where I start to switch off. So, if you're thinking to yourself 'Ugh more fancy self-help terminology', trust me I understand. Me-ology™ is more than just a word; it is a lifestyle choice. It affects the choices we make, the situations we encounter, relationships, work, parenting, and most of all who you feel as an individual. A lack of self-esteem is the monster behind imposter syndrome, anxiety, depression, and doubt. The key part of this term is self. It's how you feel about who you are as an individual (something you can never escape) and how that feeling reflects in your day-to-day life. Gaining self-esteem is about working on that frame of mind to be SELFISH.

From this moment on I'd like you to commit to changing the way you view the phrase 'it's all about me' and view it for what it truly is: a means to live your life fully, with you at the core, enabling you to flourish and be all that you can be for you and for everyone around you.

Exercise

To be yourself involves investing in YOU. We're going to start with a simple daily exercise that may feel uncomfortable at first but as we move on will benefit your mindset.

So, take a mirror and say aloud…

I love myself

I love myself

NOW SAY IT LOUDER...

I love myself

I love myself

Doesn't that feel good? You're already one step closer to celebrating you, learning to express yourself and being with who you are. Empowerment is not a magic remedy; it is a mindset that has been practiced for thousands of years.

Life is your greatest adventure. Embrace each challenge and never be afraid to live it authentically, lovingly, wildly and to its fullest.

"Pig ask him moda why him snout solong, she seh when yuh grow, yuh wi know."

Similar to my mother's saying, 'tomorrow is not promised', this saying is based on the fact that even if we understand things today, we cannot predict what will happen in the future. Things that seem one way now may take on new significance in the future, things that don't make sense now one day will.

Practicing self-esteem enables us to be mindful and purposeful, to be aware that we are always growing and to move with change not against it.

3. What is Self-Empowerment?

Self-empowerment is designed to increase our sense of autonomy and self-determination; in its truest form, it is the process which enables us to represent ourselves in a uniquely responsible and confident way.

This is a tool that I use each and every day in every single area of my life via Me-ology™. The essence of my own sense of empowerment is perhaps the most treasured gift my mother bestowed me. Though I did not realise it at the time, by raising me to have independence, confidence, and self-esteem, she was laying a foundation that would set me in good stead for the rest of my life. As I grew older, I learned how to deepen my own sense of empowerment despite life's challenges, and I learned how to share it with those around me.

"You have to expect things of yourself before you can do them."

Michael Jordan

I suppose the reason I preach and practice Me-ology™ so whole-heartedly is because it applies to both the process of self-empowerment and to the support of others. It is the route by which we are free to overcome our sense of powerlessness and lack of influence, and to recognise and eventually to utilise all of our many resources as well as opportunities.

Unlike so many other solutions in the world, empowerment is not a magic remedy, it is not a story or yarn or marketing; it is a frame of mind that has been practiced for thousands of years.

Empowerment is the bedrock for all my endeavours and efforts, no matter how different and varied they all appear on first gaze. Why? Well, empowerment means that we can all take charge of our own lives, careers, bodies, ambitions, illnesses, and tribulations.

My children will often say to me 'I can do this by myself'. From walking down, the stairs to climbing up a frame or riding a bike. That is because we are each born with an internal belief system. Over time, life experiences can make us confused, angry, hurt, jaded, rejected, inferior (the list is endless!) until we lose our sense of empowerment and start to feel less and less in control of our lives, actions and destiny.

Our legacy is the most precious thing we leave behind after we're gone, so make it a good one.

Who Am I?

Identity mapping is the flagship to the person you are. It is individually assumed from birth, whether we are aware of it or not. It's the journey we take that uses in-depth assessments to build a picture of you that identifies you in relation to others. Your identity is the key to successful inter-actions. It's what identifies and sets us apart from another.

We each develop our own according to genetics, environment, and choice. It's our unique combination of emotional, attitudinal, and behavioural response patterns. I recall my mother always reminding me to 'treat life as an adventure'. I believe that our personality is realised through our life adventures. So, if we embrace life as an adventure, we are exciting and enhancing our personality. As with any adventure we select our destination, set a route and we aim to achieve it.

So... Who Are You?

The essence of who we are at our core fundamentally stays the same but WHO we are, is adapting and growing all the time. Bereavement, divorce, a new baby, a new job, all of these and more shape who we are as we grow each and every day. If we aren't aware or mindful, life's events can shape us in ways we don't recognise or understand. In a similar sense, our personality is realised through our life adventures. When we embrace life as an adventure we are enticing and enhancing our personality to be revealed in its fullest. As with any adventure we select our destination, set a route and we aim to achieve it.

Don't spend your life dreaming of who or what you want to be...instead work at becoming who and what you want to be.

4. Belief

My grandmother would probably think I'd gone a bit mad if I spoke to her about tapping into the truest version of yourself. After all, the way we talk now is new. The thing is the generations before us were more concerned about 'keeping up appearances'. That's just the way things were done, most of our elderly were raised to never air their dirty laundry, express how they really feel and to care deeply about what the church and neighbours 'might' think. There's something admirable about their resilience, they certainly would never have plastered their business all over Facebook or been seen drunk and frolicking on reality TV. Still, we know that generation experienced a higher rate of child mortality, alcoholism was rife and mental health wasn't understood let alone talked about.

In the Caribbean community, the humiliation of the local reverend hearing about bad behaviour was enough to keep the truth behind closed doors. Many other cultures were exactly the same.

Mental health went untreated and lots of my generation grew up in mentally, physically, sexually abusive homes and had no idea anything was wrong until we entered the 1990's and Oprah got us all talking about our childhoods and our feelings. Sadly, this lack of communication and never talking about challenges left its mark. I believe that we've gone from being too closeted to telling everyone everything in the space of a few decades and that plays a part in why we constantly talk about who we 'really' are. Why do so many of us feel confused about who they really are and how did the issue of personal identity become so challenging? While it may seem like you should automatically know how to be yourself, that is rarely the case.

Belief kill and belief cure

What you believe creates your reality. Our minds are incredibly powerful machines. It's always fascinated me that we will go to A&E with an injury, but we leave our minds unchecked. Our bodies can will us to die. How you perceive your world is dependent on how you think which why inner strength and self-belief is a matter of perception.

Recollection

It's the mid-70's and a three-year old me is eagerly helping my formidable mother prepare for an event. Watching her assemble friends and allocating roles, I keenly nominated herself as a helper. As the gaze of the room turned to me, I valiantly raised my plastic cup and, addressing my audience asked assuredly, 'Drinks, anyone?'

Gregarious, confident, I was and am the product of parents who instilled in me an indomitable self-belief. I was happy and strong-willed; I flourished in a home filled with love, hugs, and an ethos of determination. By the time I'd turned eleven, I knew exactly what I wanted to be.

Separation, Breakdown or Failure?

Fast forward thirty years and I was at the top of my game. I had reached a point with my PR companies where I was the go-to for giving voice to the voiceless. I had turned down proposals and waited until I was in my 30's before I got married. I waited travelled, studied, and waited patiently until I knew in my heart, I had found 'The One'. I didn't let anything sway my decisions, having dated celebrities I wasn't impressed by the glitz and I chose someone who I believed was a good man and a perfect match for me. My aunt was married to his brother, he came from a God-fearing family, he had a great work ethic and as far as I was concerned, he ticked every box. Our connection was a deep one and my sister nicknamed us batty and bench and when we got married on a Bayesian beach, I thought 'this is it'.

As much as you feel you know someone and have the same values, life's challenges sometimes show you otherwise. When my husband's business went down the toilet, his reaction shocked me, but I did what I do well, I supported him, fought for him, and probably at times even enabled his worsening behaviour. I thought he'd push through the low times and be a leader for our family unit but instead it was a slow disappointment and he unravelled before me, hurt everyone around him and went into self-destruct mode as I tried my best to hold on to the marriage. I genuinely always thought losing my mum would be the one thing that would break me. In a weird way my marriage breakdown affected me more. My bond with my mum meant that I felt a closeness to her spirit, I felt at peace. The breakdown of my marriage didn't leave me feeling any type of peace, I felt like a failure, I felt disappointed and I felt confused. One of the worst parts of hitting rock bottom is the amount of people who are happy to see you hit it! The wedding had been a lavish beachside ceremony. I hadn't realised there were people who were secretly jealous, who were quick to look over as my marriage fell apart, not to wish me well but to say, 'Oh, so she's not as perfect as she looks/acts/seems.' I was blessed that I had many genuine supporters at that time to balance that out, most of all my mother.

Months after the marriage was over, my mum had to stage an intervention. She drove to my house, used her spare key, marched up the stairs into my bedroom and pulled open the curtains. She had never seen me defeated before and she wasn't about to let me stay in that state. Afterwards, mum asked me where this deep sense of failure came from. 'Was it your illusion of marriage you're grieving Diahanne, or the actual marriage?' She asked me. Either way, mum said it was like I had an eclipse over my sunshine. It made me question all that I believed in. The little girl who was once filled with confidence had been thrashed, and this was my rock bottom.

Now, unable to get out of bed without the deep sense of purpose that had led me all of my life. The value of time is that eventually it gives you answers. With time, I met my life partner, and I was able to see that I hadn't failed at anything; he simply wasn't the right fit for me no matter how much I thought he was and almost a decade later the universe sent me someone who is.

I grew up in a notorious estate under the watchful eyes of a devoted mother who loyally, incorrigibly, encouraged my natural ability to shine and inspire and my father, a championship boxer (I watched him work in a factory for years as he trained to later become a welterweight champion) which shaped and moulded my core values: perseverance and positivity. I had no idea that having grown and flourished as a confident woman that it could be snatched from me in one instant. I learned that our core is something we must constantly work at maintain and nurture; just like everything else that we care about. Anyone who has known me for a long time will tell you I'm still the same old Diahanne. My confidence has meant that I've always been happy in my own skin and comfortable being me. Still, there are some parts of me that have shifted, grown organically and even changed completely. My form is the same, but my shape has altered.

Exercise

Look over your growth as an individual and for a moment ignore all the people who have been alongside you. Who were you as a child? What were your dreams and hopes? As a teen? As a young adult? In your twenties and thirties? What were your strongest traits throughout those times? Write down every single part of who you were, good and bad and cross off the ones you have worked at that no longer apply. Look at what is left. Look at those things that have remained with you throughout all the stems and changes life has given you. Now, jot them down. Also take a moment to jot down those things you feel have been tainted or lost that you'd like to tapinto again. I guarantee, once you acknowledge who YOU are and who you'd like to get back to being, it will make the process so much quicker.

Although I've been through many challenges and times of significant change, some often uncomfortable, my response has always been the same - get up, stand up, and brush yourself off because the best is yet to come.

5. Forging Real Friendships

My mum often cited an interesting saying: 'blood is not thicker than water'; a healthy friendship between two balanced people is a deeply fulfilling experience. In many ways you can feel more aligned with a well-chosen friend because you chose them, unlike the family you had no choice in! I am blessed to have friends who I consider my family; as my self-esteem and inner strength has grown, these friendships have strengthened too. When we are at school surrounded by our peers it sometimes feels as though the friendships we make are for life. The reality is that as we grow older, we change, our priorities and lifestyles change and often most of those friendships fade away. I still stay in touch with some of my old schoolfriends; Living an 'All About Me' life means being particular about the types of friendships you form.

You may have unintentionally surrounded yourself with people who are not good for you, because it has felt familiar to you in the past. You may feel you owe your friend something or don't want to 'give up' on a friendship that has spanned decades. However, there are friendships we have to walk away from and what I've learned is that it's O.K to walk away from toxic relationships. It's crucial for your emotional well-being, but it's not always easy.

Over the years I have developed friends in different circles; each are valued but different because I accept that people have different roles in my life. I am proud to have a small inner circle of friends I see as my family who are involved in my daily life, who love me for me and who I can trust completely with anything I face. Don't get me wrong, nothing is always moonbeams and rainbows, but I can trust that when they tell me I'm wrong (which they do!) they are coming from a place of respect, love and sincerity, not agenda, spite or insecurity. I'm also proud to have many wider circles of old friends, new friends, old colleagues and clients, neighbours, and associates who I may not speak to everyday or share my innermost life events with, but I appreciate for the role they play in my life.

Friendships naturally go through phases. I have been with friends through marriages and divorces, pregnancies, sickness, successes, and trials. I've witnessed friends go through terrible times and forget how amazing they are, and I've been happy to remind them just as they have me. Similarly, I have learned the hard way that the moment a relationship becomes toxic, it's time to remind myself 'It's all about me', put my well-being first, and stick with it even when a friend takes advantage of you, belittles you, abuses you, steals, lies or disrespects you - it's time to be clear about your boundaries.

WRITE YOUR OWN NOTES...

WRITE YOUR OWN NOTES...

WRITE YOUR OWN NOTES...

WRITE YOUR OWN NOTES...

Duppy Know Who Fi Frighten.

This Caribbean saying is understood to mean that bullies and abusers can distinguish between those they can intimidate and those who are better left alone because they aren't easily manipulated or intimidated.

To me, this saying isn't about being weak as some people interpret it. Yes, there are many toxic people I have avoided because they sensed my inner-strength and moved on to an easier target! Yet I have also had toxic people target me because of my strengths. I learned the hard way that my good intentions to please and help others were actually causing me stress and, in some cases, it was as if the more I said 'yes', it perpetuated the problem rather than allowing people to think for themselves. I also believe that guilt played a role, as turning down people who need help can be a tough call and there are those who will take advantage of that. Developing your self-esteem, understanding red flags, and having boundaries doesn't automatically mean you never encounter, meet, date or work with toxic people just because now 'duppy knows who fi frighten', it simply means you identify it sooner, recognise it and are able to process it from a position of strength and knowledge. Years ago, I was friends with an older woman, and she became my mentor. I was humbled and thrilled to have an older, well respected woman to guide and advise me - it was exactly the feminine presence I wanted in my life to shape me. The moment she turned on me was a major learning curve because it went against everything I had ever known or received from my female elders. It went against how I viewed role models and the principles my mother taught me on 'sending the lift back down'. I didn't allow the experience to make me become bitter, however, I did accept the learning and it has informed how I treat my young mentees because I never want to make a young woman who looks up to me feel the way that I felt in being attacked, slandered, and maligned by a woman my mother's age. It makes me feel even more passionate about being a real role model and guide to young women not just those who are my mentees but those I meet through my charity or my awards event where pioneers literally 'pass on the baton' to the next generation. Bad experiences can create positive change if we have the self-esteem to allow it to shape us for the better.

I also once employed a PA who presented as a strong and very impressive woman and I had no idea she was quietly jealous in the background and working to destroy my reputation, friendships and even my family, until she left the company and then literally tried to destroy my life. My knowledge on toxic people didn't spare me from her, but it did inform how I responded. As much as I was disappointed, I was thankful that God allowed me to see who she really was before she had the chance to create any further damage and destruction. Many people present, very convincingly, as one way but eventually the truth manifests and having a strong sense of self-esteem is key to handling and processing such hurtful situations. When you see toxic behaviour for what it truly is, there's a point where you realise that other people's toxic choices and behaviour certainly is not 'All About You', but very much about them and gives yourself permission to accept the learning and move forward.

Amongst my closest friends, we are just as comfortable sitting in silence as we are chatting for hours. Your real friends know your shortcomings (and their own) and love you anyway. You are perhaps the "best version" of yourself when you're with your friends. Not because you depend on them to feel whole but because you feel as though you're utterly understood which can be a rare gift.

The lifeblood of a healthy friendship is authenticity and honesty. I'm completely honest with my inner circle of friends and I know they do not hesitate to be just as honest with me. Here's where intention plays a key part. You know in your heart when you're advising, warning or even telling a friend off, out of real concern and love; and it's important to identify when they are doing the same. For example, when "honesty" is a constant criticism of everything you do and how you do it (to your face or behind your back) the friendship is toxic.

Remember, the signs are always there, it's about listening to your gut feelings when those signs first appear. When you find yourself no longer wanting to open up to your friend because you are anxious that they will focus on the negative, make it about themselves or dismiss your feelings, it's a sign that should never be ignored.

"When someone shows you who they are, believe them the first time".
Maya Angelou

Ask yourself... Who isn't clapping? A good friend once told me when she wins an award, she notices the so-called friends that aren't clapping. Look at your happiest times and occasions. Was your friend encouraging you, helping you, supporting you along the way and clapping for you when you finally won? People who love you will be happy when you are. This is an important one because a person does not genuinely love you if they aren't happy for your achievements, big or small.

The good news is that a crisis in confidence can rock you to your core, but ultimately, it is something that is learnt and developed. A loss of confidence does not need to be a permanent state. Through positive change and by breaking old habits and adopting new productive ones, we can learn to boost our self-esteem and confidence to overcome negative experiences.One of the biggest misconceptions about healthy friendships is that you'll never disagree. That's just not true. Arguing isn't unhealthy; expressing your opinions freely might cause you to disagree from time to time and that's natural. Like so many things it's all about intention and sincerity. Real friends want their relationship to be solid, which means they aren't afraid to talk things over. The intention of the argument should be to listen, share, understand and compromise, not to 'win'. Honest communication won't allow tension or negativity to linger for long, it creates an environment where you'll both be happy to address issues, forgive and move on.

Oprah's friendship with Gayle King is highly publicised, people assume that for two women to have been so close for thirty years they must be a couple because rarely people have such close and real bonds.

Oprah: I understand why people think we're gay. There isn't a definition in our culture for this kind of bond between women. So, I get why people have to label it - how can you be this close without it being sexual? How else can you explain a level of intimacy where someone always loves you, always respects you, admires you?
Gayle: Wants the best for you.
Oprah: Wants the best for you in every single situation of your life. Lifts you up. Supports you. Always! That's an incredibly rare thing between even the closest of friends.

Sadly, it's true. Authentic relationships are rare, and that's because so many of us are struggling with low self-esteem and intent on putting ourselves second (or even last) that the old cliché 'you can't love another until you love yourself' comes to the surface which is why an 'All About Me' life is so important. My late mother was and still is my role model; she was also my best friend. She instilled key values, taught me right from wrong and gave me countless sayings that at the time never made much sense, but are now key core values that I live by today. Growing up, my mother pointed me in the direction of the likes of Martin Luther King Jr and Mother Theresa, strong characters who were concerned with empowering and transforming the lives of others.

My mother was an awesome person and I miss her every day. She was such an inspiring role model because she wanted the best for me. Her death also confirmed to me how much she inspired other people and led such a selfless life. This was evident because she was not remembered for her material possessions or her fabulous and colourful sense of style. My mother is remembered because she left an imprint, a mark on people's lives through acts of kindness and generosity and this is a legacy that I am tremendously proud to continue. The friends we choose are also a part of our legacy; if we choose them wisely and treat them well, that is how we live on.

Nuh care how hog try fi hide under sheep wool, him grunt always betray him.

No matter how a pig tries to disguise himself under sheep wool, his grunt will always give him away. The meaning centres on authenticity. Never pretend to be anything other than who you truly are because ultimately, your real self will always surface. Be your truest self no matter where you are, or else, like the pig pretending to be a sheep, your grunt will give you away.

6. Wearing Hats

'The most important thing is to be honest about yourself. Secrets weigh heavy and it's when you try to keep everything to yourself that it becomes a burden. You waste energy agonising when you could be living your life and realising your dreams'. Nicola Adams

We all wear different hats. The hat I wear as a mother is vastly different to the hat I wear today as a businesswoman. Still, they are both me. The problem is when we start to wear hats that aren't actually US at all; they are hats made for us by other people, in colours we probably don't even like, that fit badly and do us no favours at all.

Today I am the truest version of myself. I will admit that during my modelling days (when I was weighed every week and the numbers that popped up were everything) I was probably vainer that I like to admit but as time passed other things became more important. The adrenaline that made me a PR machine isn't so easily lit up, so social cause does so much more for me than footballers and £ signs ever did. That isn't because I've changed who I am; I was always passionate about giving a voice to those who need one, but I discovered a hat that fit me better and I wasn't afraid to take off the old one and put on a new and better one. The difference is that when you change your hat to please others, it rarely fits. A lot like Cinderella's stepsisters trying to squeeze their feet into her glass slipper, we can pretend to fit in or become somebody we aren't for a new partner or friend but ultimately it causes more pain than it's worth! Look back at Task 2 and look at the parts of yourself that have remained the same no matter what, it's likely those are the real you. Again, go back to that list and be creative because there may also be parts of you that you have never felt able to fully 'be'. Abusive parents, forceful or self-absorbed friends. Coercively controlling partners all have the power to mute our inner voice if we let them. Those are the truly authentic parts of you. Ask yourself this question: If you were alone on a desert island, what kind of person would you be? Without the glare of colleagues or neighbours or partners your authentic self is free to emerge. How much of you isn't real?

Remember, the things you write down are for your eyes only so be honest and recognise that in doing so you're taking the first steps towards living a fuller, realer life.

My Business Hat

I went through all my life as a young professional, feeling a sense of double discrimination as a black female. From my early modelling days to working in marketing and PR, everywhere I worked was an uphill battle. I exuded confidence, drive and determination and it was an education for me to be judged purely on my gender and race despite my ability. It was no co-incidence that I went on to become a 1990's pioneer of diversity marketing as my lived experiences had informed my choices about the type of changes I wanted to create. I can't say that every bad experience I had was from white employers and colleagues, but I can honestly say that all too often it was other minorities and black people specifically (and worst still for me, black women!) who seemed to be my greatest opposers. In my professional career I have used every experience, good and bad, to be teachable moments. For every great achievement I am proud of, there is often a challenge or hardship that inspired my companies and ventures and drove me to push even harder. That is how in an 'All About Me' life, we are the authors of our own legacy, we can choose to allow professional and educational experiences to break us... or make us.

My company '15 Degrees' was the first to specialise in diversity marketing and race relations almost 30 years ago. Fast forward to 2021 and my awards event The Baton Awards, which honours and celebrates minority women was born from the same desire to balance out the playing fields, give credit where its often due but not given, create platforms for recognition and to inspire and grow the next generation. My charity Strength With In Me Foundation came years after surviving domestic abuse and learning to speak out and inspire other victims. The list goes on but needless to say, I believe you can turn 'negative' experiences into victories at home and at work, no matter what you've experienced. I believe that anyone who works hard makes huge sacrifices.

There have been times when I refused to be 'dumbed down', change my appearance and generally 'play the game'. This has resulted in the loss of friendship and business opportunities. However, the friendships and business opportunities I have forged instead have been meaningful, lasting, authentic and with a socio-political cause. I have said on many occasions that money is not my God. If something doesn't sit with my values and my morals about humanity, I refuse to do it. Sadly, when you maintain high views and morals you often stand alone. Ultimately, I have sacrificed the 'quick wins' for the slow burn, and big money contracts for philanthropy and core beliefs. That said, after a few decades I'm still standing....

"Surround yourself with only people who are going to lift you higher." Oprah Winfrey

The people I surround myself with are central to who I am and what I do. I believe I am a winner, so I surround myself with people of a winning mentality. When I see people chasing their dreams, it gives me motivation to keep chasing mine.

Never mistake this for rubbing shoulders with the 'right' people or 'networking' because its deeper than that. Seeking and maintaining connections with positive, authentic, and principled people is a huge part of getting ahead in business because as they say it's often not what you know, but who you know. If everyone around you has money and fame but they are greedy, selfish, and vain, they can't possibly truly benefit or elevate you on your professional journey. So often I ask people to tell me about themselves and they tell me what they do. Life isn't about our job titles; its about our core values, our passion, purpose and principles.

I don't just surround myself with peers from the same background with the same views and life experiences. I surround myself with people whose energy is contagious. The people I spend time with may be older than me, younger than me, be from a different race, religion, or life journey – but they all have character, depth, and purpose and that inspires me to be and do better professionally and personally.

Abraham Lincoln said: "Reputation is the shadow. Character is the tree." Our character is much more than just our reputation. Our reputation is what we try to display for others to see. Our character is who we are even when no one is watching. Having a good character means doing the right thing just because it is right to do what is right.

Life is your greatest adventure. Embrace each challenge and never be afraid to live it authentically, lovingly, wildly and to its fullest.

Living Well, Being Well...

I never underestimate the effect that health has on our lives and how it has the power (if we let it) to change us. I've known people who have become recluses because of illness and in the process lost every part of themselves that they liked most. Here's the thing, accepting and loving who you are and the package you come in IS part of your health. A positive emotional self-image makes us feel better, which releases serotonin and positively impacts our bodies. Have you ever noticed the 'glow' that newlyweds have? That doesn't just come from having a new spouse, it comes from all the positive energy, love, and beautiful energy; your confidence is through the roof, the sun is shining, and you are loved. Why wouldn't you be glowing? You can have your very own 'honeymoon glow' whenever you choose; all it takes is for us to inhale and LOVE the person we see in the mirror, hold onto it tight and exhale.

Recollection:

I'll be honest and tell you that I have always been blessed with amazing health. Back in my 'high flying' days, I was up early and out until late, I lived on airplanes and in hotels and even so much as a flu irritated me because it slowed me down and my life was 150 mph. In my 30's, along came a word I didn't know much about. Grief.

Lessons Learned

After my mum's death I experienced an onset of sudden, unpredictable, and debilitating bouts of symptoms that brought fatigue, and muscle pain. I felt as though my body was attacking me. I felt my confidence slip away with the hair loss and the extra 20lbs that appeared and wouldn't shift. I felt anger at the irony of always being such an energetic and active person now forced to lie down when there's so much more I want to do, feel, and see. I felt completely exhausted and like the ultimate betrayal, my body was attacking itself.

Here's the thing. In a strange way, my health suddenly declining after years of impeccable health, actually made me realise the importance of living a life that's 'All About Me.' My body reminding me of my limits has never been fun, but it did force me to revaluate. Before my mum died, I had always divided myself up into a hundred pieces. I did, after all, work in the fast-paced world of PR for two decades as an expert and I could probably impress you with some of the celebrity clients I have had over the years, but the problem was, they stopped impressing me.

The world of showbiz became too shallow, too meaningless, and vain. My new perspective made me more and more aware of my mortality and I didn't feel I was contributing to the world in a way that would carve out a legacy. You could say I turned my back on that world in search of something MORE. Yes, my PR company is still, I'm happy to say, a booming global company but the difference now is all my clients have a social cause and they come to me to help them make a real impact in the world. Losing my mum made me more particular about what, and even who, I give my time to and my legacy became more important than how many zeroes were at the end of a cheque. I can't deny that the knocks in my life also mean my confidence has been shaken. My hair isn't as thick as it used to be. I never thought I'd stay the same as when I was 21 but change isn't always easy to accept. Still, bit by bit I am learning to love this new body.

Wha inna darkness muss come a light.

What is in the darkness must come to light. This means the things that we try to hide will be revealed in the end. The key to authenticity is to live a life worthy of scrutiny, so that you will never need to be ashamed of any part of it. I've travelled the world and discovered it's smaller than we think! Treat everyone with respect and be true to who you are.

Never be ashamed of your scars. They serve as a reminder of your battles and the proof that you have survived.

7. Being Perfect

The pressure to be perfect. I don't conform to societal demands, but I am part of that bubble. I'd be lying if I said I wasn't; being on screen in front of the camera, speaking at events where hundreds of people are looking at me has at times taken me right back to my modelling days of being physically scrutinised.

With age and time, I've learned to identify how much of a myth the 'perfect woman' idea is. Over the years, I've stopped trying to live up to other people's standards of 'perfection'. I've been blessed with enormous gifts and successes in my life, but I've also faced hardships, loss, and unthinkable challenges. Years after each of my challenges, after the storms had passed and the silver lining had emerged, I've asked myself: 'what would I change?', if there were a genie in a bottle somewhere would I rub it and ask to have been given 'the perfect life?' Absolutely not! Every experience I have had has made me who I am today. Every hardship has given me perspective, wisdom, and moxie. Through loss I've learned to appreciate what I have. Through heartache I've learned what I'm made of. I've discovered for myself the gloriously 'imperfect' womanhood that my own mother taught me with her actions, words, lifestyle, and legacy. Lessons learned, sometimes the hard way, that I can now proudly bestow my own children. I can't promise them life will be 'perfect', but I can instil within them the tools to be graceful, courageous and patient. I can teach them how to embrace and love their own perfect imperfections, how to expect the best but prepare for the worst and how to stand up, perfectly, when life knocks them down. Perfection' is something we can only try to carve out for ourselves depending on the standards we set for ourselves. Real perfection is what we make of it, not what we are told it should be.

My life hasn't always folded neatly into boxes with bows on, but it has been something of an adventure. My deepest lows have taught me how to seek out and appreciate the dizzying highs. During my career I've met all kinds of people who (on the surface) appear to have it all. I suspect that on the outside there have been times I've been perceived in much the same way. And if there's one thing I've learned it's that almost nothing is as it appears. Lady Diana was envied by thousands of women for decades before we learned the truths behind her own story; one that was rid-dled with bulimia, insecurity, loneliness, and rejection.

As women we should celebrate our 'flaws', appreciate ourselves in all our precious wonder. From stretch marks to failed marriages, the car that doesn't always start and that stubborn 10lbs that just won't shift. Perfection is not what house you live in or how glossy your hair is. Perfection is what you make of life. Or rather, what life makes of you. It's what you do with the cards you're dealt, with the mistakes you've made, with the hardships you've overcome. It's to open your heart and mind to the universe and see what it delivers to you. To wake up every day and be the best you can be to love and be loved. To set yourself authentic standards and to go to bed each night knowing you've done your best to meet them. It's to accept that life events are, for the most part, beyond our control. To accept a higher wisdom, to know there is a bigger picture.

Lessons Learned

I've fostered many children but when the twins came to me, I just knew it was going to be different. By the time they found me, I was a different Diahanne. I had survived domestic abuse, lost my mum, been divorced and more. I always thought I'd have kids of my own and that is sometimes the irony of life as a woman. I married the man I thought was the man of my dreams and would be the father of my children. After the marriage imploded, I realised why so many divorced and separated women in their late thirties feel robbed of motherhood, or as though they have given their best years away, wasted their best years and more. Of course, it doesn't help that often the same man who wasted your 'window of fertility' can go on and have children until he's 100 if he chooses!

Thankfully, with time I realised I had been spared the experience of raising a child with someone who, as I discovered, had very different values to me. Thankfully, I learned that sometimes being a parent comes in many forms. It's not about blood or the term the child calls you but the role you play in their life. The curveball came when I finally met someone that I wanted to spend the rest of my life with and I knew that if I wanted to have children with anyone, it was him. It was quite a wake-up call being told I was pre-menopausal… early menopause at that! I never thought by the time I finally met my life love that it would be too late to have children and for a short time I mourned that lost window of opportunity. If there's one thing I've learned, it's that the universe takes, and it gives. My life now, with my life partner, both sides of our close-knit families, our circle of friends and of course the twin girls, is a rich life. It may not be what some consider traditional (and what does that look like in 2021, anyway?) but I'd rather be happy in an 'unconventional' setting, than unhappy in a conventional one.

Lessons Learned

Looking at my mother's life, talking with family, talking to her friends and her work colleagues, I can honestly say that my mother lived a life that touched so many. That's such a precious thing; I believe that we are all on this earth to give something to the world, whether it's behind closed doors or in the public eye, it's still significant – it's still your mark, your purpose, your legacy. What are you here for? What am I here for? Whatever the answer I'm going to focus on my goals and my purpose and if I can be half the woman my mother was known to be… beautiful, intelligent, kind, caring, supportive, entertaining, sociable… all of that and more, then I would be leaving, as she did a legacy to be proud of. Let's strip it back to basics: what will your legacy be? It may sound morbid, but this thought will focus your energies on the things that really matter, and it will hone your attention on creating it. This is all it takes to create a legacy. The beauty of this is that it sets a pace for 'perfect imperfection'; carving a legacy takes the focus off of your weight (I'm yet to see an obituary that celebrates someone being a size zero) and anything else that distracts from your living legacy and places the focus on the time you spend with your children, the conversations you have with loved ones. These days I'm more likely to wake up and call my friends to tell them I love them than run for a manicure because my quest to leave behind a meaningful legacy has that effect. I believe it's so important to leave behind a beautiful legacy. We may not all have a national fan base; but we all have someone. And if just one person reminisces and remembers you as an authentic and kind person who gave back and remained true, in good times and bad. That is more than enough in my book.

Exercise

This exercise is to write your own obituary! Some people find this an uncomfortable task but it's a real revelation. What would the people you love have to say about you? Use this space to start designing your own legacy. You can write your own obituary, or you can simply try to imagine what your loved ones would have to say about you at your funeral. I know this seems like a morbid job, but it really does open our eyes to what really matters. What would you like to be remembered for and who would you like to be remembered as? I'll bet the answers don't include cars or jewellery but the things we know are everlasting. Take a long look at your list.

If you died tomorrow is that the legacy, you'd leave behind? This method has the effect of making you want to get out there and start today.

Unfortunately, we won't all live to receive our letter from the Queen. Sometimes, believing we have another fifty years that pushes us to live a life that isn't actually all about the right things. It's believing tomorrow might be our last that forces us to pick up the phone, say the things we've been putting off, and start becoming the person you really want to be.

Its not only about grasping life with both hands in terms of seizing opportunities, chasing dreams, and often so much goes unsaid and efforts go unsung until a person dies? We seem to think we will have more time, but the truth is the time is always now. Live an 'All About Me' life every day, and as youcreate your legacy never be afraid to tribute, acknowledge and express love and appreciation to the people who inspire, support and influence you. seeking your own personal brand of fulfilment; it's also about celebrating the people who inspire you. I feel that all too often we don't celebrate and acknowledge our champions until they are gone.

'I made millions during my career, and now at the end of my life all I can think is... I wish I had been true to myself...'

Anon

WRITE YOUR OWN NOTES...

WRITE YOUR OWN NOTES...

WRITE YOUR OWN NOTES...

WRITE YOUR OWN NOTES...

WRITE YOUR OWN NOTES...

WRITE YOUR OWN NOTES...

There are always flaws and imperfections that can be found when looked from a different point of view. Flawless is simply an adjective used to describe everything good in this world. So, accept, acknowledge, and celebrate who you are. That way no one can use them against you. Here are 5 tips to help you on your way:

1. View your perceived flaws in a whole new light. Nothing is ever completely good or completely bad.

2. Be ever grateful. Make yourself a 'Gratitude Box'. Regularly write down something you are grateful for and place it in your box. Review it daily.

3. Recognize that you are not always your thoughts.

4. Be vulnerable with others.

5. Look after and appreciate your individuality, you may be different – but that can only be a good thing!

"You must have an aim, a vision, a goal. For the person sailing through life with no destination or 'port-of-call', Every wind is the wrong wind."

Anon

**Practice the following positive
self-affirmations daily:**

I believe in myself unconditionally.

I welcome love from myself.

I am at peace with where I am.

I embrace who I am.

I am comfortable, just as I am.

I own my own love.

I am whole.

I am constantly becoming my best self.

8. Achieving Happy

"Happiness is not a matter of intensity but of balance, order, rhythm, and harmony."

Thomas Merton

Some years ago, a palliative nurse named Bronnie Ware recorded the most common regrets of the patients she worked with in the last 12-weeks of their lives. She wrote about the phenomenal clarity of vision that people gain at the end of their lives and how we can learn from their wisdom. Common themes emerged so many times that she was able to narrow them down to just five.

They were:
1. I wish I'd had the courage to live a life true to myself, not the life others expected of me.
2. I wish I hadn't worked so hard.
3. I wish I'd had the courage to express my feelings.
4. I wish I'd stayed in touch with my friends.
5. I wish I had let myself be happier..

Ware said that most of her patients didn't realise until the end that happiness is a choice. They didn't realise that living an 'All About Me' life was even an option until they only had weeks left. Being happy is something everyone craves in life, the holy grail of the happily ever after. I often hear people say or sometimes sigh, "But I just want to be happy…" But what exactly does that mean?

Happiness is one of those fuzzy words that is so subjective, it means so many different things to different people. For me, being happy meant taking a good long hard look at my life and the choices I had made. I needed to challenge my thinking, to make sure I was really living my life on purpose and was not being driven by any hidden agendas. Sometimes we can go through life full of 'if only' as if they determine our happiness. If only I was a size 8, I'd feel so much better about myself; If only I got that promotion, I'd be able to buy a bigger house; If only I made more money, I'd be happy; If only he loved me, I'd be happy. The interesting thing that I've noticed is this – when you do eventually achieve your 'if only' and tick it off your list, it is automatically replaced with another one, whether it has made you happy or not. This tells me that if you are either making a lot of excuses or you're waiting for a positive event to happen in your life to make you happy. Either way you're wasting your time. Simply because, if you're not already happy within yourself, no amount of material stuff, wealth or people will make any difference. A little nugget I learnt was this, real happiness begins with changing your mind-set. I was reminded of this recently whilst watching an interview with Bishop TD Jakes, explaining his 5 keys to happiness. He spoke about several things, such as owning your own happiness; challenging your story by speaking positively about yourself; to enjoy the journey and not just the destination; make your relationships count and finally, balance work with play. Some of these really struck a chord with me, and looking back, I can honestly say I've been genuinely happy when these key areas are in alignment.

And let's not get it twisted, I'm not against any form of retail therapy or treating yourself to make you feel better, what I'm saying is it's about learning to be happy in the skin you are in and know your own value. I know for sure that I would not be standing today, content and at peace, without my faith in God and the relationships that I have in my life. My mother used to always tell me that no-one is an island, and this statement is so true. Nothing productive or fulfilling has happened in life without relationships. Yes, I work hard, I'm focused and passionate about a lot of things, but without family, friends, and mentors to support, laugh and cry with me, the story would have been very different. I've also learnt to appreciate the journey that I'm on, as I know I'm definitely a work in progress. The challenges, the highs and the out and out disasters, are all part of my journey and ultimately make up my story. I make a point of celebrating the little 'wins' along the way and take time to reflect on those periods where I still need to grow and learn how to do things better. Finally, all work and no play, really does not make Diahanne not a fun person to be around. So, I make sure I take time out for myself. I put myself on my own calendar. Time to reflect, pause and rest. I take time out, so that my life has balance. These are the things that bring happiness in my life. The things that make it possible for me to smile and laugh throughout the mess that people don't even see.

This is because true happiness is within; it really is an inside job. It's not in our careers, in cars, in money or even people. So, taking responsibility for my happiness starts with me, it is ultimately my own business. While I am minding mine, I strongly recommend you do the same. Be happy. That is the true meaning of living a life that is all about YOU.

RIP Caroline Elizabeth Rhiney (Mummy) Sunrise 30.06.52 – Sunset 24.01.10

I've been thinking about life. Sadly, my mother has died, and I was reminded, like a rug being pulled from under my feet, that 'tomorrow waits for no man' or woman. We laugh, we cry, we have sad times, we have good times… our life experiences are endless, but as I asked in my previous blog… do we appreciate each day? Now more than ever I appreciate what today brings, because it's a fact tomorrow isn't promised to any of us.

Legacy is enduring; I believe that we are all on this earth to give something to the world, whether it's behind closed doors or in the public eye, it's still significant – it's still your mark, your purpose, your legacy. What are you here for? What am I here for? Whatever the answer I'm going to focus on my goals and my purpose and if I can be half the woman my mother was known to be… beautiful, intelligent, kind, caring, supportive, entertaining, sociable… all of that and more, then I would be leaving, as she did a legacy to be proud of. Two things that have helped me during my loss … one, is the memory of knowing that my mother and I always said, 'I love you'. As a word of advice if you can help it don't part with a loved one on an argument.

Recollection

My mum bought a sunny yellow Datsun with her own money and it marked the end of her relationship with my Dad. This was the beginning of my education in human relationships; what it means to have a choice to give up your own happiness for someone else's.

My mum kept her car and drove it around with pride, its bright and happy colour making her unmissable in a traffic line! I couldn't help but admire her bravery. My Dad would now tell you he was being silly, that he had been so afraid to lose the love of his life that he became threatened by her independence and tried to control it. My mum was not willing to sacrifice her happiness and I'm so proud that she didn't. Little did we know that she would die at such a young age; buying her Datsun was just one of the many things mum may never have had the time to do if she hadn't grabbed life by both hands.

"Once we achieve true inner-strength and self-belief we are able to be the best version of ourselves. This in turn leads us to make better choices, overcome challenges with conviction, feel independently happy whether we are alone or with others, and ultimately helps us to be a source of positive energy for ourselves and to our loved ones."

9. Loss And Legacy

Sometimes life will throw something at you, like losing a job, the end of a relationship, a betrayal or discovering that things haven't been as you thought they were. These are the things that cause you to question your decisions, your judgement, even your values. Suddenly every area of your life is challenged or compromised.

This is what a crisis of confidence does. It stops you in your tracks, pulls the rug of everything you were confident in out from under you and makes you doubt everything you do or have done in your past. It is as if your personal landscape involving meaning has changed, which in turn takes away your ability to trust your own thoughts and feelings. This then makes room for the negative belief that you're simply not good enough to deal with life in general. So how does this crisis of confidence occur? I would say that this is something that affects everyone as we transition through various stages of life. You may have gone through a stressful or challenging time and a negative incident happens that feels like "the straw that broke the camel's back". It may or may not be a big event, but nevertheless it becomes your tipping point. Before you know it, your normally confident attitude plunges into self-doubt and anxiety. This crisis in confidence usually leaves you feeling disoriented at best and frightened at worst.

In most cases you are left feeling negative or shameful. The negative narrative will convince you that you are a failure or inadequate and you begin to lose faith in yourself. You may find you are constantly self-critical or holding yourself to unrealistic high standards. When this occurs, try to look at the evidence in your life that counters the negative expectations of yourself, or the internal pressures to be someone you're not. In other words try and discover your successes, or the things you achieved that were good enough. Then reframe your negative beliefs and thoughts along more positive, compassionate, and realistic lines. When you have a confidence crisis, don't despair, instead, start to use some of these confidence-boosting techniques:

Give yourself permission to regain confidence

Remind yourself who you really are - a person of integrity and worth. Remember what you appreciate about - yourself and get in touch with your ethics and principles and what you believe. Recall the positive feedback you have received from people who care about you and whose opinions you respect. Try and reconnect with your passions and dreams and if they have changed create an updated version that reflects the new you.

Change your language

The language you use can profoundly affect your mood and belief in yourself. This is an area that you can control by talking to yourself using positive statements such as "this is a temporary setback"; "I've had many more successes and better times than the pain and doubt that's happening now".

Forgive yourself

The ability to accept and forgive yourself, combined with compassion for the distress you are experiencing are pivotal turning points for successfully dealing with a crisis in confidence, and regaining faith in yourself.

Evaluate your relationships

Assess the relationships in your life. Do they support or sabotage you? All relationships change with time; some get better, some get worse. If you have relationships in your life that are more of a burden than a joy, it may be time to sever your ties - or at least loosen the reins. Identify people that have the qualities you admire - people you feel you could learn from and who could learn from you, as well. Additionally, look at starting new relationships with people you can have fun with, as boosting your confidence can be fun too.

Seek professional help

Some people may be more vulnerable to a crisis in confidence than others. If you grew up in an environment that was devaluing or unsupportive or if you find yourself drawn to people who neglect or abuse you, consider connecting with a counsellor who can provide additional support to build your strength and draw healthier lines around your relationships. The crucial thing is once you recognise the signs of this type of crisis in confidence, you are better placed to deal with it when the time comes. It is also important to understand what you have learnt about yourself and what changes you may need to make in your life or relationships. Try to establish what made you so vulnerable in the first instance and what you could do to build yourself up?

The impact of loss cannot be underestimated in its effect on our self-esteem. The word itself means to no longer have or to have less of something and in losing someone or something important we are left feeling like a 'shell' of our former fuller self. To me, loss feels as though life has just thrown a huge curveball. Things are moving along just fine and then the giant; dark cloud of grief swallows you up. At times, loss can make you feel as though you've lost yourself to the point where you begin to wonder if you'll ever feel carefree, happy or just 'the old you' ever again. It takes so long to piece yourself back together again that at times you wonder if it's even going to happen! You ask, 'will I ever feel whole again?' If you have been thrown the curveball of bereavement, I am sorry for your loss. I am also confident that it will not stop you from reaching your fullest potential to be the best version of yourself. There is no fast remedy for loss, it is a process that demands our attention for as much time as it takes. If loss has knocked your self-esteem, I can't fix that for you, but I can offer you some perspective.

Recollection

My mother was a beautiful, vibrant, and strong woman who collapsed suddenly with a brain aneurysm and never woke up. I felt that my world had ended. One day later we made the horrendous decision to turn off her life support. There were no goodbye's or last words, just the sudden and unexpected death of a healthy woman. Over 1,000 people turned up to her funeral, all of them with a story about 'just how lovely' she was: for me as her child, the hole she has left behind is indescribable. Whenever Mother's Day comes around, people often ask me how I feel without my mother. I always say I can only describe it in one way: imagine you have lost an arm. You have had to learn to operate and function every day without a crucial part of you. You have a stump that reminds you of the arm you once had, so there's always that reminder that a major part of you is missing no matter how well you adapt.

You adapt enough to remember that lost part of you with a smile. Still, there are moments where I feel I've lost her all over again especially on occasions like Mother's Day which just remind me what I've lost. My father was devastated by the death of the love of his life. My mum had two girls and a boy. We all had the same loss, but we each grieved completely differently. I was faith driven, my brother bottled up and he, with my sister, became angry. This is why I say this isn't a 'one size fits all' situation, even when you each come from the same womb the process of grief is unique. At times I felt alone in my grief because of this although ultimately and eventually the experience brought us closer together.

Before mum passed away, I went through a separation from my then husband and the pain was awful, at the time I thought it was the worst pain I could feel. The person who came and pulled the curtains up and told me to get up, was my mum. So, when she died as we were going through a divorce, the pain of her not being there at the other end of the phone or to shake me out of my grief was gone. I used to dial her phone and listen to her voicemail so that I could sleep. My mother died when I was, as the Americans say, 'grown'. Yet the profound feeling of losing my mother made me feel like a child. The vulnerability, the nakedness, the feeling of walking around lost is unforgettable. I felt as though I would never be the same again. After my mum died, I felt as though I had lost my protection. Some of the worst experiences of my life happened after my mum died and I just couldn't believe the timing; how was I meant to navigate my way through such huge challenges without my best friend? I sometimes wonder how my experience with my violent former partner would have been if my mum had been alive.

"I really think a champion is defined not by their wins but by how they can recover when they fall."

Serena Williams

Lessons Learned

Imagine my surprise when I discovered this wasn't the case. there is life after death. You will truly smile again; I don't know how long it will take but you will. You will take your wedding ring off. You will eventually clear out boxes and boxes of clothes, go to places you would have sworn you'd never visit again and play the songs that once filled you with sadness with a smile instead. I don't believe that the wound ever really heals, I believe that we adapt to it and eventually you reach a point where you no longer wake up in the morning and jump out of bed to escape your own thoughts. You will reach a point where every tiny memory doesn't evoke pain or guilt or that crushing pain that only someone who has lost a close loved one truly knows. You will go places and do things you never imagined possible when you were bawling from a part of your body you'd never felt before on the kitchen floor. You will break boundaries you didn't even realize you'd created and learn you CAN feel whole again, just a different kind of wholeness. Where there is loss, there is also gain (something I never thought I'd say) and in the years since mum has died our family has grown. My daughters came into my life when they were two-years old and have bought me so much joy; they made me realise how selfish (in the usual sense of the word) I was before them and how much more there was to live for in the years after my mum.

Nieces and nephews and great-nephews and great-nieces have been born and I see bits of mum living on in all of them.

I've grown into a whole new human being on so many levels that I thought were impossible after time had seemed to stop. I'd like you to consider the things you've lost in your life. Not everybody has experienced bereavement yet, but you may have lost something you treasured in a different way; the husband you loved or the friends you had no choice but to cut off. It may not even be a person; losing your house or job can be deeply traumatic. Next to this, write down everything you felt you lost at that time. Then write down another list; a list of everything important that you have gained and next to them everything you gained with it. This isn't about replacing or anything, so be honest. I think you might be surprised to see that whatever you have been through, there has been more growth and joy than maybe you realise. This task tales' complete honesty, please don't feel guilty about listing all the good things in your life post-loss, the good elements in your life are just as real and noteworthy as the painful ones. Chances are that your gains are more than you realised.

If that's the case, take some time to ponder this. It's amazing to think that after the hardest times in your life that anything good can happen ever again but that's just it, when we start to invest in ourselves the process often reveals positives that we just haven't stopped to really notice. Keep adding to these lists every week and be creative.

10. Raising 'Generation Confident'

I have had hundreds of children in my care; none were from my womb but each of them was woven into my life as though they are my own. Most, like all children, have flown the nest to live out full lives, some are still with me and some of them always will be. I have fostered hundreds of children and I believe I've won awards for it because I nurtured each one as my own. Trying to raise confident children isn't easy. The moment I became a parent, I knew that unless I was strong within myself, it would be hard to raise the happy, healthy, confident children I instantly wanted them to be. I'm still learning, and I believe it's important to take your children on that journey with you. As you grow and thrive, so will they.

Recollection

It's the Christmas school play and after a long week of practising, my foster child (who loves to sing and dreams of appearing on The Voice one day) stood at the front of the stage and projected her voice, smiling at the audience. Another parent approached me to say 'Wow! Your daughter was SO confident up there!' It dawned on me that the two key bits of advice I'd given her (smile at the audience and project your voice) had gotten through; all the hours of listening to her practice the songs and all my belief in her ability had paid off. I couldn't help but ponder on how many of my friends and clients have talked about not being supported and listened to at home and the effect this had on their long-term self-esteem. As a parent, our own sense of self-esteem will reveal itself if we aren't actively working on our inner strength, likewise the benefits of nurturing your child's confidence are so profound they will provide you with such a deep sense of joy and accomplishment that your own self-esteem will be better for it.

Communicating Positivity

It's so key to try and see things from your child's perspective. However, much you may not understand something a child has said or done; it doesn't mean there isn't a reason. If we dismiss or reject our children's feelings, opinions, and ideas with "don't be silly you're too young to know what you're talking about" "that's a ridiculous idea' they will feel invalidated. If you've ever had a difficult conversation with someone, you'll know that feeling shuts down communication. Empathy allows our children to feel heard and understood which helps them to feel confident. Clear, candid, confident communication means that you express your feelings, needs, and wants effectively, while respecting others. Aggressiveness is a sign that you aren't in control of your emotions which is confusing for a child and puts them on the defensive, and like a mirror image eventually they will act aggressively back.

Healthy Distance

I honestly believe it takes a village to raise a child. I can't imagine who I'd be today not just without my parents but without all the aunties, uncles, friends and more who helped to shape me. I trust my inner circle to influence and shape my children and I'm happy for them to communicate in a different way to me. To coin another phrase, no man is an island and I'm proud to say my daughters have grown up surrounded by aunts and uncles who share the same core as me but have their own stories and opinions and lifestyles. I love the fact that my daughters tell me everything as I have always had a 'no secrets' rule in our home but I accept that as they grow they might prefer to call one of their trusted aunties or uncles and I welcome that. It's not a failure to open up your parenting approach with the people you trust; it's a strength to put your child's wellbeing before any insecurities or possessiveness you might feel.

Similarly, passiveness gives children a disproportionate amount of control. Feeling confident in your new All About Me life is being assured in your ability to parent with control, respect, empathy, and authority. When you communicate assertively, use "I" statements, openly but appropriately discuss your feelings, and give reasoning for your boundaries or rules, you teach a child how to do the same. In communicating with a child who is still growing and looks to you to set the example, assertiveness means being consistent but always keeping your child's feelings, needs, and wants in mind. This builds mutual respect. Teaching your child how to communicate assertively and considerately is an important life skill for them to have. One day they will leave home and must speak to their boss, colleagues, landlord, plumber, and doctor on their own and we as adults know how challenging all those things and more can be on a daily basis. Healthy relationships are a core part of Me-ology™ and I always say, this begins at home. Positive communication leads to nurturing relationships, understanding, and feelings of worth. A child who can recognise a healthy relationship can readily recognise a toxic one and have the strength to voice their boundaries; there are so many instances where this is vital.

Positive communication focuses on respect for the child and involves both speaking and listening. Communication is what we say and how we say it and as I often say, 'it's not what you say, it's how you say it'. How many times have you unintendedly said something and caused offence? Communication takes consideration especially in children because poor communication can lead to kids who "turn off" adults (and all authority figures), aggressive conflicts and bickering and feelings of worthlessness.

Anyone who has met my daughters will tell you they certainly aren't afraid to speak their minds! The moment my twin girls arrived I knew I wanted them to be confident, outspoken girls; I also knew I didn't want that to be at the expense of good manners and being respectful.

Authentic Parenting
I knew I could never be the type of parent to put on an act around my children. My own mum managed to be communicative, open, genuine and command the respect

of her children and I wanted to achieve the same. It's an ongoing journey and I don't always get it right! Children need genuine connections like plants need water. It's a must. For a child to healthfully develop into his or her best self, there must be a place in their life where they feel safe, honest, open, trusted, and valued. School may not always be that place.

Sometimes learning centres have very narrow views of intelligence, talent, and creative freedom to express your true self. I certainly never understood learning sex education from catholic school nuns in 5th grade - it didn't make sense to me. Educational systems often have many of these paradoxes alive and well. Mindfully creating an authentic parenting and personal style that fosters the best from you and others is a process. Keep at it. This work is extraordinary. It is your legacy. Through learning to use your emotional rudder well you simultaneously teach this power to your children (and their children and so on).

Understanding

The core of parenting should always lie in nurturing children to have a healthy self-image and self-esteem as they are vital to success. Not just academically, but emotional success, it's a gift that once you've instilled it (unfortunately there's no manual!) your child will reap the benefits. A big part of that means accepting children the way they are sporty or booky, quiet or loud. As parents we must give our children the opportunities to push their comfort zone, challenge their reservations, expand their horizons as this is all confident boosting. They should just always be done with a respect for who your child is at their core, even if it seems to be constantly changing. Young people who have had their individualism genuinely accepted (which is quite different to indulging a child's every whim!) tend to grow into confident, outgoing, self-assured adults. Forcing children to fit into a prescribed mould nearly always backfires.

It's important to work to identify your child's self-esteem and work with them to build up those areas. Set aside some time to sit and go through this exercise with your child; you might just be surprised how much you'll learn about them in the process.

"Life is like riding a bicycle. To keep your balance, you must keep moving."

Albert Einstein

11. Achieving Balance

I know one thing for certain; the more balanced I feel, is the happier I feel. I think I can safely say the same applies to us all. What does balance really mean? To me, balance is defined by having a firm grasp of all the elements in our lives. I think it's about feeling clarity, conviction, contentment, and focus. When all the compartments of our lives are in harmony and each complement each other, balance is the feeling that makes us feel as though we are 'in the right place'. The foremost elements of our lives typically comprise work, relationships, hobbies, and interests. Ironically, these are the external elements that cause us the most stress and yet also cause us to pay less attention to what is going on internally. So, here are my top tips for striking this vital balance between mind, body, and soul in practical ways.

Accept and Acknowledge

Take a deep breath and focus on your positives. List as many of them as you can think of and be proud of them; once you identify them it not only boosts your self-belief; it also helps you to hone and sharpen that area. This process helps you to love what you see, rather than what others do, or do not see.

Plan and Prepare

Turn off your iPhone, iPad, or tablet at least twice a day, and be mindful. It's important to create a peaceful moment where you can be alone and take time to breathe deeply, meditate or just sit quietly. This allows you to clear your mind. You can then take notice of the environment around you, reflect on your daily experiences, and appreciate those things that are of importance to you. Additionally, it also allows you to bring closure to the events of the day. Being mindful in this way, combined with mediation has been shown to reduce the symptoms of anxiety and stress.

This is a little like going to the gym, only for your mind. Switching off and reflecting in silence is a treat for your mind, which is overloaded by a constant stream of thoughts all day. Treat your mind to some silence on a regular basis to balance it out and boost your happiness and sense of peace.

"The best motivation always comes from within."
Michael Johnson

12. Be...And Beyond

Setting aside your fears and inhibitions requires loving yourself completely and reaching out of your comfort zone. Focus on mind, body, and soul and how you can nurture and cleanse all parts of you. We need to release negative energy otherwise the build-up of stress can lead to negative thoughts, poor self-esteem, frustration and even pain, which are just as toxic as substances that can send your body into overdrive. Long periods of stress, anxiety and depression can lead to an increased risk of diabetes, stroke, and cardiovascular disease. Recognising the signs and symptoms of stress and negative tension can be a lifesaver. It will help you figure out ways of coping and save you from adopting unhealthy coping methods, such as drinking or smoking.

Although there is no quick fix (because no single method works for everyone) the key is to release the tension and reduce the stress. Whether it's as simple as having a good cry, relaxation, meditation, prayer, an exercise session or a good laugh with friends, this release can energise your mind and body and help you move on. Balance is something that is within your grasp. Once you prioritise yourself on every level and start putting time into your wellbeing above and beyond everything else, you will quickly reap the benefits.

"God gi yuh two ears and one mouth fi a reason."

Listening and Observing is Golden

Having healthy self-esteem makes it easier to listen more than you speak because you feel at ease within yourself. On a deeper level, words have power and should always be used wisely because they represent who you are on the inside.

The Importance of Setting Goals

Everything has a beginning, so I'll start by saying: If you've ever asked yourself 'Why are we here?' you will have already invested into an essential key to your life. Think about it for a moment......Why are we here?

If you were to ask that question to a room full of people you might be surprised at the many and varied answers from: to live life to the full and enjoy it despite its ups and downs; to give praise and thanks to life; to become fruitful, successful, to be a mother etc., but however we answer that question determines the state of our mind and self-worth. From the time you knew how to say your name (and trust me some of us have names that could qualify for the Guinness Book of Records) you became an individual, recognising your very being.

A life without meaning is no life at all. I strongly believe in God however we chose to interpret it. For me what is important is as human beings we do not enjoy a given meaning from an existential perspective. As such, it is up to each and every one of us to create our own meaning, our own reason for living.

The precious gift of life from God gives me the freedom and free will to find my own path in life. It's true some of us walk the high road, some the high street and some end up in the cul-de-sac even though they have access to their own destiny, my Mother always echoed the words: 'to gain the most of your life, you need to give of yourself to others first.' As imperfect human beings, we have an innate selfishness which we arm ourselves with for protection or defence. Tapping back into this is the purpose of this book, but it's true to say that we are in an unfavourable position to help others if we cannot satisfy ourselves first, so having a purpose or goal in life is the key to a successful future.

The biggest single thing that gives us a purpose, other than jobs, partners or children is GOALS. Whether we choose to believe and work with it, we all have a purpose in life. Some recognise it from an early age, some may even deny it, and some are still looking for it ……like trying to find the elusive right foot of the gladiator sandals at Primark – it's hard to find sometimes but it's there.

"The end of each day is a time to look back and reflect on those moments in which we have truly shone. Not only that, but to seek to continue to do so. To thank those around us who have shone their light when we may have found ourselves in darkness, and the hope that they will continue to be a beacon."

Exercise

Make **SMART** choices by measuring success in these 5 ways:

Specific

Measurable

Attainable

Relevant

Time-bound

The thing about goals is that they are unique to everyone and can change according to our circumstances. But to the setting of goals is a format that works for all realisms and which I have personally tested. As a child I always knew and believed I wanted to influence people in some way. The path I went through may not have dictated this in an obvious way as I started my career as a model although you could say this did have a big influence on the people around me. I always wanted to help people empower themselves and have been successful in motivating people, especially women and youth through workshops, mentoring, motivational speaking; all the things I do now.

If I didn't have a goal, I can honestly say my world would have been so much different and I believe sadly that many people simply get 'lost in translation' because of a lack of purpose and/or goal in life. Mum once said, "*A woman without a goal is naked and exposed to life's elements.*" Our family life was full of fun, laughter, sharing, caring and this became so evident in our unique role as mothers, sisters, aunts, grandmothers – we all have an inherited template to produce 'good fruitage' through positive goals.

"I'd rather be a 'could-be'
if I cannot be an 'are';
because a 'could-be' is a
'maybe' who is reaching
for a star. I'd rather be a
'has-been' than a
'might-have-been', by far,
for a 'might-have-been'
has never been, but a
'has' was once an 'are'."

Anon

Whether it's finding a suitable partner, land the prefect job, raise successful children…. the right guidelines are essential, using the 5 SMART ways of measuring success: Specific, Measurable, Attainable, Relevant, Time-bound. Successful people are focused people who know what they want and what they are working towards. It's critical to ensure you have a measurable goal in life and take control of it with both hands. Aim for 100% and you may score 90% or more. Settle for 70% and you may average the minimal. Where do you see yourself in 5, 10, 15 years' time? This is the classic interview question – for good reason. Why? It immediately shows whether you are a 'goal-getter'. Do you want to have moved onto bigger and better things, or are you happy to stay precisely where you are now? Do you want to have a successful career, a happy and healthy home life, money in the bank, great holidays, the respect of others, good friends? Then it's time to start building.

Express your goals positively: 'Execute this technique well' is a much better goal than 'Don't make this stupid mistake.'

Be precise: Set a precise goal, putting in date, names additional information so that you can measure achievement. If you do this, you will know exactly when you have achieved the goal and can take complete satisfaction from having achieved it.

Set priorities: When you have several goals, give each a priority. This helps you to avoid feeling overwhelmed and directs your attention to the most important ones.

Write goals down: This will crystallize and give more force.

Keep operational goals small: Keep the low-level goals you areworking towards small and achievable. If a goal is too large, then it can seem that you are not making progress towards it. Keeping goals small and incremental gives more opportunities for reward. Derive today's goals from larger ones.

Set performance goals, not outcome goals: There is nothing more dispiriting than failing to achieve a personal goal for reasons outside of your control. In business for example, these could be bad business environments or unexpected effects of government policy. If you base your goals on personal performance, then you can keep control over the achievement of your goals and draw satisfaction from them.

Set realistic goals: It is important to set goals that you can achieve. All sorts of people (employers, parents, media, society) set unrealistic goals for you. They will often do this in ignorance of your own desires and ambitions. Alternatively, you may set goals that are too high, because you may not appreciate either the obstacles in the way or understand quite how much skill you need to develop to achieve a level of performance.

Save money: Set up a standing order of £50.00 each week into a subsidiary account that you cannot easily access. Don't spend your life dreaming of who or what you want to be... instead work at becoming who and what you want to be. Intention is the proof of will. It determines the journey toward the goal. The intention is the 'why 'behind our actions.

One of the greatest gifts of value I believe we can give someone is to help them conceive possibility into their imagination. Through understanding that 'this is possible, and this is possible for me,' can open up an entirely new path in a person's life. I truly believe that those of us, who are able and equipped, have a responsibility, a duty to help those less well off than ourselves, as there is no greater satisfaction, than seeing those that used to stumble, stand tall and shine. Life is a great adventure. Embrace each challenge and never be afraid to live it authentically, lovingly, wildly and to its fullest.

I know by experience that mental health can be debilitating and destructive and I put myself in the picture here as I'm not ashamed to say I suffered mentally during the experiences I have shared with you. Even though I am a qualified psychologist, with each challenge I realised no woman is an island; I too needed help if only to keep myself sane!

I sought counselling for many months and let me tell you, I had no qualms about giving up buying a pair of the latest Manolo Blahnik's for the price of buying some peace of mind. Was I being kind to myself? Yes. Was I taking my life too seriously? Yes. And that I think is the problem with too many of us – we take life too seriously which only leads to more stress.

There's so much negativity around us that if we take it all on board we would explode under the pressure. And sadly, we only need to walk down our local high street to see some negative behaviour no doubt precipitated by negative news. Whilst some of us do need professional help, we can all empower ourselves through regular MOT's. We do it for our car, our teeth, our pets – so why not for our mind? In all these circumstances we shouldn't wait for the symptomatic issues before we seek help. As my dear mother used to say: "prevention is better than cure".

Over the years I've learned the hard way how to trust myself more, to act on my beliefs and understandings, to allow myself to try new things based on my journey and how to listen. How to listen to my circle, to my heart, body and spirit. Life is too short. That's why I put me on my own calendarand weigh out my Year because even in my worst years there has been lots to be thankful for. I take time out, so that my life has balance. Taking responsibility for my happiness begins with me.

Negativity is toxic to your entire physical, mental, and emotional system, so clearing negative energy is an important strategy on your journey of holistic well-being. Here are six ways to remove negative energy from your mind and body.

1.   Practice daily meditation to help you witness your thoughts rather than being caught up in an interpretation or evaluation. This process will heal and restore your entire system to balance and positivity.

2.   Get out and observe nature. This is a powerful and practical way to reduce negative energy from mind and body by recreating a 'system reboot' acknowledging positive creativity around us.

3.   Move your body by performing yoga techniques, running, brisk walking. Physical activity helps purge negativity from your system on several levels and keeps you fit at the same time.

4.   Go complaint-free. Not easy in today's care-free world but it has the benefit of reframing your mind-set. Complaining is linked to self-pity and both negates your responsibility for self-worth.

5.   Smile often. Simply put, smiling makes it difficult to sustain a negative mood.

Practice the following positive affirmations – daily.

I deserve love.

My own love is superior.

I love my body and all that it does for me.

My imperfections are what makes me unique.

I will always choose me.

I am exactly who I need to be.I am special.

"Nothing can dim the light which shines from within."

Maya Angelou

Gran: Liccle But Tallawa

When we got the call that mum was dying, we all assumed it was Gran. Mum was so young, vibrant, and full of life, it hadn't occurred to any of us she could go before Gran. When Gran walked over to my mum on her death bed, she said 'your children should never go before you'. Her decline came soon after mum died and it was us, her grandchildren who became her carers. I believe she died of a broken heart; (my mum had sold her house to live with and support Gran, so after mum died, Gran walked past her room everyday) each time I took Gran to an appointment, the doctors would say it was like she had simply given up. The deterioration of my Gran was prolonged but when she eventually died, it felt so terrifyingly final to lose two generations of women, to become the family matriarch overnight. It was a huge loss; Gran was the one whose shoulders we stood on.

The stories she told about St Kitts, the life she had lived after migrating to England, raising children, bereavement. Gran taught me what resilience was. After my grandad died suddenly in an accident when I was five, I watched her in awe as she continued nursing, being the rock of the family and her courage was remarkable. The legacy she has left behind is a giant one, not a day goes by when I don't quote things she said or see myself in her sense of humour and dynamism. She really was liccle but tallawa. Losing my mum and then losing Gran really emphasized the importance of womanhood and sisterhood for me. Their anecdotes, life lessons, unforgettable quotes, stories all stopped when they died and whilst I had the memories, they were no longer there for me to ask questions or gain live perspective. I've spent much of my life creating global sisterhoods of women who share, inspire, celebrate, and empower each other and in so many ways my passion stems from both my mum and grandma, what they stood for, and the things I miss about them most.

13. Collectively Made

Community is important. If it weren't for the people around me when I've needed help, I couldn't have achieved as much. I don't believe that anyone can make a difference alone, which is why I constantly collaborate. To coin a phrase, it takes a village.

I don't believe in the term 'self-made'! Simply because no matter what our individual journeys have been like, we are all the culmination of the people and experiences that have shaped us, good and bad. We are all collectively made. Success is something that takes time, dedication, and hard work. Very rarely, does someone achieve it in isolation. It takes support from others. My mother always used to say: "no one is an island or ever accomplishes much on their own." If success is defined by having people who believe in us, encourage us, and cheer us on, it takes a collaborative effort for each one of us to be successful.

I've seen so many times when people who achieve success, the ease at which they forget where they came from or who helped them on their way. Once we get to the top, we can forget what it took to get there and even perhaps forget the people that are still where we used to be. When we become successful, it is important that we support those coming behind us to also be successful. Once we get to the top, we need to 'send the lift back down' to give those behind us support to get to the top too. We must not fear competition and we must be careful of having a 'crabs in a barrel' mentality as there is plenty of room for all of us to be successful. It is because we are collectively made that the more successful each one of us becomes, the better off we will be as individuals and as a collective. Every tiny drop of water combines to create a force as powerful as the ocean.

So, as I said, the gun was on the back of my head, I had heard the safety release, the click of bullet being released and, in that moment, I knew it was over. It wasn't. The bullet had jammed, and as I ran for my life down the stairs and out the front door, I thanked God for my life and have thanked Him every day since. I lived to tell this tale.

I am no longer the Diahanne I was before that night; I am no longer the same Diahanne I was before my mum died, before my marriage breakdown - each loss has moulded me. I am also not the same Diahanne I was before I was a mother, a foster carer, a charity founder and so many great moments in my life. Both good and bad have shaped me, re-shaped me, and shaped me again. I've no doubt the next decades of my life will continue to shape me. I'm still a work in process and will continue to be until the day I take my last breath. But, what I'm committed to be is the best 'all about me' for myself, family, friends, colleagues, clients, team, mentees, mentors, ancestors, and legacy. My wish for you reading this is to be the author of your own story and legacy. Life is rarely perfect and I'm sure there are many of you who have experienced just as much loss and growth as I have, some of you even more than I can imagine. By surviving each challenge, you have gained a library of rich experiences. We cannot control the events of our lives, but we can control how we respond and make a choice to allow challenges to grow and shape us. So, no matter where you are in life, I wish you growth, success, self-esteem, real friendship, self-realisation, and that at the end of this book you have some of the tools to begin a new chapter in your life, one that is entitled 'All About Me.'

"Be balanced, be whole, be you... and shine bright."

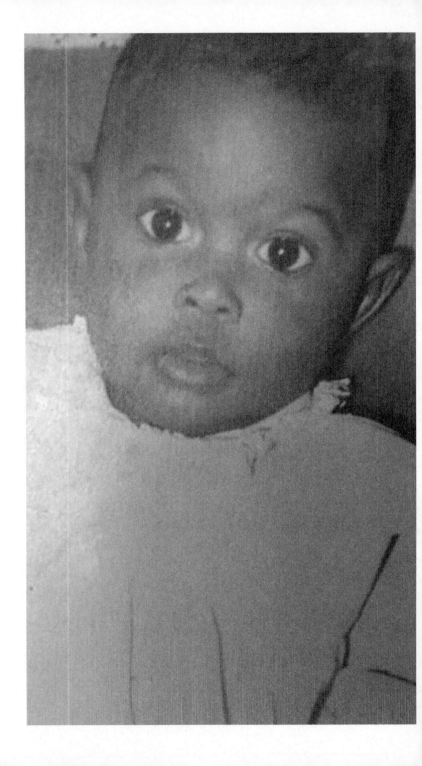

Resources and useful links

The Baton Awards:

https://thebatonawards.com/

Met National Helplines:

National Domestic Abuse Helpline:

https://www.nationaldahelpline.org.uk/ 0808 2000 247

Domestic Violence Assist: https://www.dvassist.org.uk/ 0800 195 8699

Women's Aid Domestic Violence 24-hour National Helpline: https://www.
womensaid.org.uk/ 0800 2000 247

Need to Know:

LONDON, Jan 14th 2021 British pharmacies launched a codeword to tackle
a feared spike in domestic violence during lockdown, telling victims to "ask for
ANI" (Action Needed Immediately) at the counter to secretly summon help.
You can travel during lockdown to escape domestic abuse.

Apps for teaching relaxation and well-being techniques to ease symptoms of
anxiety and related health conditions and disorders: Calm, Headspace,
Breathe2Relax and Happify.

Rights of Women: Rights of Women provides legal advice and information to women affected by violence. https://rightsofwomen.org.uk/ 020 7251 6575

Samaritans: Samaritans provides a confidential support and advice service which is open every single day of the year. https://www.samaritans.org/ Free 116 123 – Samaritans Self-help App

Victim support: Victim support is an independent charity which supports people affected by crime or traumatic events, including domestic abuse. https://www.victimsupport.org.uk/ freephone 08 08 16 89 111

Refuge: Refuge provides a range of services to support abused women and children. https://www.refuge.org.uk/ Freephone 24-Hour National Domestic Abuse Helpline: 0808 2000 247

Shelter: Help if you're homeless: domestic abuse. https://england.shelter.org.uk/ Supporter Helpdesk on 0300 330 1234

Domestic Shelters.org: – recommended books on domestic abuse survivors: https://www.domesticshelters.org/resources/books/abuse-survivor-stories

Books

Good Vibes, Good Life by Vex King

Cognitive Behavioural Therapy by Olivia Telford

The Subtle Art of Not Giving a F*ck by Mark Manson

Speak Your Truth by Fearne Cotton

How to Win Friends and Influence People by Dale Carnegie

Leading on Empty by Wayne Cordeiro

Surrounded by Idiots by Thomas Erikson

The Mansion on the Hill by Fred Goodman

The Purpose of Power by Alicia Garza

No Win Race by Derek A Bardowell

Outliers by Malcolm Gladwell

The Tipping Point by Malcolm Gladwell

Black Box Thinking by Matthew Syed

Bounce: The Myth of Talent and the Power of Practice by Matthew Syed

Start With Why by Simon Sinek

Think and Grow Rich by Napoleon Hill

The Power of Now by Eckhaart Tolle

The 7 Habits of Highly Effective People by Stephen R Covey

Rich Dad, Poor Dad by Robert Kiyosaki

The Road Less Traveled by M Scott Peck

The Four Agreements by don Miguel Ruiz

The Seven Spiritual Laws of Success by Deepak Chopra

The Alchemist by Paulo Coelho

The Habits of Highly Effective People by Stephen R Covey

Why Should White Guys Have All The Fun by Reginald F Lewis
and Blair Walker

The Audacity of Hope by Barack Obama

Becoming by Michelle Obama

We Rise Speeches by Inspirational Black Women by Michelle Obama

Printed in Great Britain
by Amazon